MW00885759

What Is the Best Place to Visit?

by Mrs. Wilson's
and Mrs. Kennemer's classes
with Tony Stead

capstone
classroom

There are so many wonderful places to visit.

Here are some favorites from two different second grade classes.

South India

There are many extraordinary places in the world to visit. I think the best place to visit is South India.

South India is sensational because the views are so beautiful that you can just stand there looking at things like the mountains. The volcanoes are very pretty and stupendous.

If you like animals and hiking, try a jungle safari. You can see animals like panthers, tigers, monkeys, peacocks, goats, and deer! The safari is astonishing. Try hiking too! You can see birds.

The shops are in clusters, but the clothes are beautiful! The jewelry is usually silver, gold, or diamonds. Be careful with them; they're very delicate. Accessories like scarves are there too.

Now that you've read this, you may think that South India is stunning. To me, I think it's amazing!

by Nisha

North Carolina

In my opinion, the best place to visit is North Carolina. Here are some reasons why I think it is such a great place.

North Carolina is fun because when my family was there, we rented a stupendous house in Chetola. It was right next to the pool and park. You can meet new friends. In the pool, you can have fun with your family.

If you are an adventurer, you would love to go to Grandfather Mountain. There you can go to the zoo, which has mountain lions, birds, cute monkeys, and bears. One of the bears was rescued. She has three kids. Grandfather Mountain also has a swinging metal bridge that stretches from one mountain to another.

If you look down, it is 5,305 feet! When you get to the other side, you have a great view!

Chetola has really fun paddleboats. You pedal the boats to a beautiful waterfall. The pedaling is good exercise! I enjoyed gazing down into the water. We go to Chetola annually.

North Carolina is a wonderful place. The weather is nice almost always.

by Madalynn

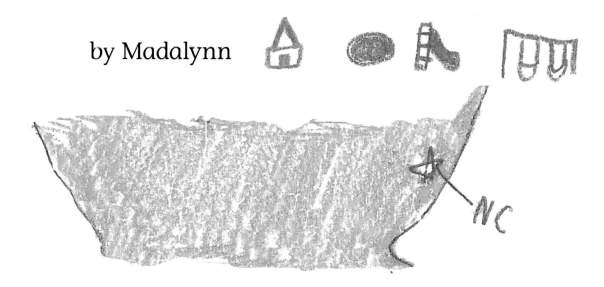

Australia

With so many great places to visit, it's hard to choose just one. But I think Australia is one of the best places to visit. I will explain why.

If you want to go somewhere amazing, then go to Australia. Would you believe that in Australia you can go on a safari? On a safari, you can see lots of animals like kangaroos! Also, the weather in Australia is hot and dry. I think these things make Australia a good place to visit.

The next time you feel like you want an adventure, ask your parents to take you to another country. Australia is a place you will definitely want to visit over and over again.

by Piper

koala

kangaroo

emu

Washington, D.C.

Washington, D.C., is a very unique place, in my opinion. I think it is the best place to visit.

One of the reasons why I like Washington, D.C., is because there are a lot of tours to take. One of my favorites is the White House tour. Other tours you can take are through George Washington's home and the Lincoln Memorial.

When you are in Washington, D.C., you can rent a bike. There are also bike tours. Sometimes you can just bring your own bike.

Washington, D.C., is a famous city because of the presidents. They also make the laws there. I recommend you go there.

by Ainsley

washington D.C.

Sanibel Island

In my opinion, Sanibel Island is the best place to visit. I will explain the reasons why I think it is so brilliant.

I like it because of the beach. It has an abundant amount of shells and very warm sand. The beach has cool water and large waves. There is also plenty of space, and I think it is always warm.

fruit

spaghetti

pizza

fish

Food

eggs

cake

lasagna

chocolate

I also like it because of the ice cream and other food. The ice-cream shop has lots of flavors. The ice cream is very yummy. The restaurants have almost every type of food you can think of. Some restaurants even sell fast food!

Another reason I like Sanibel Island is that they have really comfy beds at the hotels. You can also see the city lights and have a nice view of the beach. The hotels are very relaxing, and they even have indoor pools and yummy brunches! You should go today!

by Neha

South America

If you need a vacation after working so hard at school, then I recommend visiting South America.

The longest river is the Amazon River. You can go mountain climbing. You can also see all the amazing animals on a safari. South America is definitely a terrific place to visit.

South America's weather is warm at the top of the country because of the equator. In the middle, it will be perfect weather for you. On the bottom, it is pretty cold so you might want to bring a sweatshirt.

If you want a place with perfect weather, South America is the place to be. And don't forget your sunglasses!

by Logan

Some children chose places that have interesting monuments or natural wonders. Some think the best place to visit is far away. Others think the best place is one where they can relax with family.

Now that you've read about all of these unique places, what do you think is the best place to visit? Why do you think so?